Dedication

For all the friends and supporters of THE GREAT
HEARTLANDERS SERIES who understand the importance of
providing children the opportunity to learn about their
local heroes.

Acknowledgements

Special thanks to Betty Dixon and Shirley Rapp for their
careful attention to detail.
Sandy Beaty for research assistance and valued advice.
Chad Wall and the Nebraska State Historical Society for
their continuing help in providing excellent photographs.

Book production and layout by Acorn Books, Kansas City,
Missouri.
Cover Design: Shirley Harryman, Stonehouse Studio,
Kansas City, Missouri.

Photo Credits:
Nebraska State Historical Society, pages 10, 17, 20, 32, 40,
44, 48 and 80.
Courtesy of Hampton University Archives, page 54.
United States National Archives and Record Administra-
tion, pages 13 and 82.
John Parkison, page 98.

Dr. Susan LaFlesche Picotte, Omaha tribe.

Every day I receive letters imploring my help....As for myself, I shall willingly and gladly co-operate with the Indian Department in anything that is for the welfare of the tribe. But I shall fight good and hard against...anything that is to the tribe's detriment, even if I have to fight alone, for...I owe my people a responsibility.

Contents

A word about words:

The delineation of one's heritage is important. Consequently, everyone who worked on Dr. Picotte's biography gave careful consideration to the proper terms used to talk about the people in the book. Referring to someone as "white," "Indian," or "Native American" does not, in the final analysis, adequately, or even accurately, describe an individual. Today, many people prefer the term "Native American," but during Dr. Picotte's life, the word "Indian" was widely accepted. In fact, Dr. Picotte used the term to describe herself.

⊰ 1 ⊱

Night Visitors

All night the wind howled around the little farmhouse. It beat against the windows and rattled the doors. At times, Susan thought the roof would peel away like the skin from a buffalo carcass. A fine, frozen mist tapped on the windowpane. The sound reminded Susan of fingernails – tap, tap, tapping on the glass – as if someone were trying to claw his way inside.

Susan buried herself further under the blanket. The fireplace embers had long since died, and the chill in the air, sharp as a bowie knife, found its way through the slightest opening in the covers.

Susan listened for her sister's breathing. A faint sound, soft and familiar, came from the other side of the bed. Marguerite was sleeping soundly.

Susan tried to sleep, too. She closed her eyes and took three deep, relaxing breaths. Just yesterday, she had gone to her father and said, "I can't sleep. Night comes, and I only toss and turn. I think about what I did during the day – or didn't do. I plan what I'll do the next day. Sleep just seems to get in the way of living."

"Sleep is a feast for your mind," Iron Eye told his daughter, "and a medicine for your troubles."

Iron Eye was half white. His father was a fur trapper named Joseph LaFlesche, Sr. While growing up, Iron Eye (called Joseph LaFlesche by white people) lived mostly with his Indian family. But he also traveled with his father up and down the Missouri River, hunting throughout the territory and visiting many towns, such as St. Louis and Bellevue. When Iron Eye was about 30 years old, Chief Big Elk of the Omaha adopted him. The old chief's natural son was sickly, and Big Elk wanted someone who understood the white people to lead the tribe. After Big Elk died in 1853, Iron Eye became head chief of the Omaha. Everybody came to him with their problems.

Susan had also gone to her mother, One Woman, called Mary Gale by the white people. "I can't seem to rest," she told her mother. One Woman handed Susan a broom. "Sweeping is very restful," she said.

The howling wind pounded against the window. The glass shuddered as if it would break. Across the room, Susan heard Rosalie, another sister, turn over in bed.

"How can anyone sleep in this commotion?" Susan wondered. Off in the distance, she heard a muffled pounding.

"The horses are pacing in the corral," she thought. "They don't like this wind either." Again she closed her eyes. She was about to take another deep breath when she noticed the pounding was getting louder.

And then it was quiet. Even the wind hushed. Only a tiny whistle of air rippled along the window frame. Susan peeked out of the covers.

A face, dark and distorted, was pressed against the windowpane. A pair of hands slapped on the glass. The thick fingers spread out like a spider web. Susan choked back a scream.

In the next instant, someone banged on the front door. And then Susan saw her father hurry down the hallway, followed by One Woman carrying a lighted lantern. Iron Eye was headed toward the front door.

"Who comes?" he shouted.

The banging stopped.

"White Swan, your Ponca brother," was the reply.

Susan ran acroos the bedroom and peered down the hall.

3

Marguerite sat up in bed. "What's going on?" she asked. She and Rosalie, also awakened, scampered across the room to join Susan.

They watched Iron Eye open the door. A cold gust of wind blew in. One Woman's candle flame sputtered and almost blew out. In the light's glow stood two Indians, White Swan and Chief Standing Bear, the great Ponca leader.

Susan slipped down the hall and quietly stood beside her father. She could see beads of frost clinging to the men's eyebrows.

Iron Eye ushered the night visitors inside. One Woman rekindled the embers in the fireplace, and Susan helped by gathering kindling. She knew better than to walk in front of the visitors – that would have been rude – but she wanted to see and hear everything. Susan never liked to miss the center of

activity. Iron Eye motioned for the men to sit down. Chief Standing Bear shook his head. He pointed to the door.

"Others," he said.

Iron Eye opened the door again. One by one a line of Ponca – two dozen men, women and children – came into the house. They gathered around the fireplace. Some of the Ponca children huddled around Susan's sisters who stood by the wood box.

No one spoke. To ask a person his business before he was ready to share it was impolite. So Iron Eye waited and while he waited he silently offered his hospitality – a chair to sit on, a drinking gourd to drink from, a blanket to wrap up in.

The Ponca and Omaha had always lived near each other. Through the years many members of the Ponca and Omaha married each other. And so the two tribes were closely related. Susan once heard Standing Bear say that the Ponca and Omaha had lived side by side on the prairie for two thousand years – years of peace and friendship, he said.

Two years earlier the U.S. told the tribe – almost 600 Ponca – that they must move from their ancient homeland in northern Nebraska and the Dakota Territory. Chief Standing Bear tried to talk with the Indian Agent. He pointed out that a treaty in 1858 between the United States and the Ponca established the tribe's reservation boundaries. The treaty insured the Indians had the right to their Nebraska land "for as long as the waters shall flow." But in 1877 the government decided to give the Ponca Reservation to the Sioux. So U.S. soldiers took the Ponca to the Indian Territory, today called Oklahoma.

Word reached the Omaha that the soldiers drove the Ponca like cattle, forcing tired and hungry women and children to march at gunpoint. Many of the tribe became sick after the 500-mile journey to the Hot Land, the Indian name for the south.

And now twenty-five Ponca were back in Nebraska sitting in Iron Eye's house. "How did they get here?" Susan wondered. "And where are the others?"

At last Standing Bear spoke. "We cannot live in the Hot Land," he said. "The earth there is sickly, full of rocks and short, twisted trees. Nothing can grow. Not a spear of corn. Not a child."

"We heard of much hardship," said Iron Eye. "Much suffering."

"More than 150 of our people are dead," said White Swan. He added that many died of what the soldiers called malaria. One of those to die was Chief Standing Bear's oldest son.

"He was my last son," said the Chief. "As he was dying he begged me to take him, when he was dead, back to our old burying ground by the Swift Running

River, the Niobrara. I promised. I have put his body into a box and I have walked 80 days to return with him and many others."

No one spoke for a long time. Finally Iron Eye asked, "Will you go back to the Hot Land?"

Standing Bear shook his head. "If I stood in front of a great prairie fire," he said, "I would pick up the children and run to save their lives. If I stood on the bank of a flooding river, I would take my people and flee to higher ground. We will not return to that killing place. I will send for the ones we left behind."

"Then you may stay here until you can move again to your homeland," said Iron Eye. "Build your homes, raise your crops, and make your living among us. Our land is your land."

This was unheard of. Different tribes often hunted across the same territory, and sometimes they met together for great powwows, but they did not live together. Even tribes as friendly as the Omaha and Ponca always maintained separate communities. And then there was the U.S. government: the law said that Indians could not leave the tribe's reservation without permission, nor could they buy or sell any-thing without permission. Certainly no Indian was allowed to offer sanctuary to runaways.

Iron Eye had spent his life trying to teach his people the ways of the white man. He believed passionately that the Indian way of life was rapidly passing into history. In 1876 the U.S. government created a law forbidding hunting of the buffalo. Hunting buffalo was always central to the Indian's way of life, but Iron Eye believed that the Omaha now had to find other ways to make a living.

Many Omaha disagreed with him. They called Iron Eye's farmhouse and the other frame houses built by Omaha Indians the "Make-Believe White-Man's Village." They wanted to live the old way, pitching their tents in a circle around a common campfire.

But Iron Eye never wavered. He sent his children – five daughters and three sons – to the reservation's white school. He encouraged everyone, including his family, to call him by his white name, Joseph. He planned to enroll his daughters in the Elizabeth

Institute for Young Ladies, a school in New Jersey. In fact, Susan and Marguerite would leave for the east coast in a few months. He insisted that the Omaha learn English. He also created a police force, the first Native American force on the Great Plains, to make sure that his people did not drink alcohol. Drunkenness was destroying many Indian families and tribes throughout the American west.

Susan loved and admired her father, but sometimes she didn't understand him. On the one hand he insisted that Indians live like white people. On the other hand he would ride off to the Indian Agency and fiercely complain if he thought the U.S. government was not honoring parts of the treaty. In retaliation, the U.S. government stripped him of his rights as chief and replaced him with a "reservation chief."

Of course, Iron Eye continued to lead the tribe because his role as chief was inherited as Big Elk's adopted son. It was not something the white man could give or take away.

Although Susan was only 13 years old, she knew very well that openly challenging the rules of the white man – inviting the Ponca to live on the Omaha reservation – was extremely dangerous. It might even cause the entire Omaha tribe to be sent to the Hot Land.

Iron Eye (Instamaza in the Omaha language) was Susan's father and the last head chief of the Omaha tribe. White people called him Joseph LaFlesche.

⇥ 2 ⇤

Goodbye, Prairie Home

Everyday Susan expected to hear galloping horses and to see soldiers riding over the crest of the distant hill. But many weeks passed before they came. On the day the soldiers appeared, the Omaha and Ponca women were standing in the fields, planting. The men were constructing a new house in the Make-Believe White-Man's Village. Susan and Rosalie were leading the Ponca children in a lesson about the English alphabet.

The soldiers arrested the Ponca and took them to Ft. Omaha, 70 miles south of the reservation. Chief Standing Bear and the other leaders were put in prison.

Soon afterwards, Iron Eye called his family together.

He said to them, "If the Indian can be made to leave his lawful home and be forced to live in a land

11

not of his choosing, then what is to protect that same Indian from being forced to live in a prison, with four walls and iron locks? It is the same thing. We must find a way to defend our friends – for when they have done with the Ponca today what will stop them from coming after the Omaha tomorrow?"

He told his family that he knew many good white men and that they would help in this important cause. However, Iron Eye did not speak English very well. He spoke French and several Indian languages, including the Sioux dialect that was the Omaha language. Therefore, he would take Susan's oldest sister, Susette, with him to Ft. Omaha. She had already graduated from the Elizabeth Institute and could speak and write English very well. She would be his translator.

In the days ahead word came from Ft. Omaha. The Ponca had decided to sue the United States for violating their rights as expressed in the 1858 treaty. Iron Eye and several white people who wanted to help the Indians found two attorneys to represent the Ponca.

When Iron Eye and Susette returned to the Omaha reservation, they told everyone about the first day of the trial.

The Ponca were brought into a courtroom. A crowd gathered. Thomas H. Tibbles, assistant editor at the *Omaha World Herald*, had rallied to the Ponca's support and a huge number of white people came out in support of the Indians' cause.

The attorney representing the U.S. government stood before the judge. He announced that the Ponca could not sue the United States. He said Indians did not have the same rights as white people who could travel and live where they wanted. The Ponca had no rights, he said, because Indians were not people.

"We're not people?" Susan asked. "What are we then, cattle?" She spoke first in English and then in Omaha to make sure that Iron Eye understood her angry words. Maybe her father's opponents in the

These are Ponca. Standing Bear is in the middle. He is sitting, the third person from the left.

tribe were right. Maybe trying to live like white people was wrong. Why try to live like people who would never accept you as an equal? "What will they do next, herd us all into the Indian Territory and see to it that we vanish like the buffalo?"

One Woman clapped her hands at Susan, a sign that the girl should hush. Susan knew that she was dangerously close to insolence. Of all the daughters, Susan was the most headstrong and assertive.

"Not all white people agreed with the U.S. attorney," said Susette. "Many were against him. Several called out 'shame, shame' when he spoke. The trial has just begun. We have to wait until the final judgment. Father and I will return to Ft. Omaha in the next few days."

Susan knew that her father's desire to help his people create a new life in a white man's world had cost him dearly. Many years before her birth, he and other Omaha leaders went to Washington, D.C. and signed a treaty. The Indians agreed to give up most of their land – 43 million acres. For this land, the U.S. promised to protect the Omaha from their old enemies, the Sioux, and to pay the Omaha money, called allotments. For several years, the government did not pay the allotments. When winter supplies dwindled, many Omaha went hungry. Iron Eye used his own money and property to buy food for the tribe.

None of these hardships dampened Iron Eye's determination to lead his people toward the future. He told the Omaha, "Look ahead and you will see nothing but the white man."

Iron Eye stood by the fireplace. He had been riding for three days and did not want to sit down for awhile, he said. He had not looked at Susan while she spoke. Now he turned to her.

"It will please me that you go among the white people and learn from the best of them," he said. "You will then bring that learning to our people."

Susan said, "How can we learn anything from

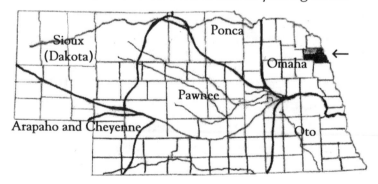

Many Indian tribes lived in Nebraska before white settlers arrived in the early 1800s. The Omaha once occupied more than six million acres. After the 1854 treaty with the U.S., the tribe agreed to live on the 300,000 acres highlighted next to the arrow. In 1865, the Omaha sold the upper portion of the reservation to the Winnebago tribe.

them when their government says we aren't people?"

"We will learn from them," he said, "not because they think one thing or the other thing about us. We will learn from them because that is the only way our people will have a future."

Both Iron Eye and One Woman wanted their children to prepare to live in the new world of non-Indian people. One Woman was the daughter of Nicomi, an Omaha-Iowa woman, and Dr. John Gale of the U.S. army. She lived briefly in St. Louis as a little girl and learned about white culture.

Susan didn't object to learning. In fact, she loved school. She and her sisters learned everything the teachers could teach them at the agency school. The family spent many months finding the money for Susan and Marguerite to attend the Elizabeth Institute.

"You will continue with your studies," Iron Eye said to Susan and Marguerite, "and will prepare to leave for the school in Elizabeth, New Jersey. There is good to come from all of this. I may never know it but you will – if you are prepared for the many changes ahead."

Susan wasn't afraid of changes. And she was never one to back off from a challenge. She raced her pony as well as any boy. When the agency teacher needed someone to call on for recitation,

Susan's hand nearly always shot up first. Susan looked forward to the challenge of Elizabeth Institute.

For weeks before the trip, she had a hard time sleeping. In her mind, she packed and repacked her bag; she studied maps so she could plot her journey; she read everything she could find about Missouri, Illinois, Ohio, Pennsylvania and New Jersey – all the places she would travel through on her way to the east coast.

Only one thing made her hesitate. How could she live and study among people whose government claimed that she and other Indians weren't people? She knew the white people at the mission church and at the U.S. Indian Agency near her home. Many were outraged at the government's position against

This is Susan's sister, Marguerite LaFlesche. She attended school on the east coast with Susan.

the Ponca. But these were white people who lived near huge populations of Indians and knew them personally. On the east coast, where white people greatly outnumbered Indians, her people were an oddity. The east coast was the center of the U.S. government and its power. Could Susan really learn anything worthwhile from people who were ruled by an authority that said she was no better than cattle?

Iron Eye said that she needed to focus on white people who were good and honest – and there were many, he said. But in the long run, he added, it didn't matter what people thought of her. Her future and her people's future depended on learning to live in this new world.

Iron Eye was her father and he was chief and Susan would do as he said. But even so, she had doubts. And then one day, Iron Eye and Susette returned from Ft. Omaha and the Ponca trial.

Judge Elmer S. Dundy, the judge in the trial, had made his decision. A huge crowd filled the courtroom to hear his ruling. Most of them hoped to see the Ponca win.

Judge Dundy said that Indians are most certainly people.

"I have never been called upon to hear or decide

a case that appealed so strongly to my sympathy," he said. "The Poncas are amongst the most peaceable and friendly of all the Indian tribes...If they could be removed to the Indian Territory by force, and kept there in the same way, I can see no good reason why they might not be taken and kept by force in the penitentiary at Lincoln, or Leavenworth, or Jefferson City, or any other place... I cannot think that any such arbitrary authority exists in this country."

And then the judge ordered Chief Standing Bear and the other Ponca to be released from custody. At that moment, as a newspaper reporter said, "such a shout went up as was never heard in a courtroom."

And many miles north, in the home of Chief Iron Eye, another shout of joy went up when the news was told.

Susan's brother and sister, Francis and Susette ("Bright Eyes") LaFlesche, toured the U.S. on behalf of Standing Bear and the Ponca.

❊3❊

A Strange New World

Susan didn't know why people sometimes called a train an Iron Horse. It was nothing like a horse. A horse stopped and started at the rider's command. Except for the thud of its hooves and an occasional snort, a horse was quiet as a butterfly compared to a locomotive. That monster machine belched when it started, clattered when it ran, and screeched when it stopped. It was like riding inside a tornado.

And, oh, how Susan loved it! At first, though, the new adventure was scary. What if she lost her ticket? What if she got off at the wrong stop?

For the first several miles, Susan and Marguerite huddled together, arm in arm. Every bump sent shudders through Marguerite; every curve made Susan's heart flutter. Marguerite said she just knew that the giant, unwieldy machine would fly off its tracks and crash in a ditch.

But soon the two girls were laughing and playing
games. Who could count the most windmills? Who
could spot the first church steeple? As the train
moved east, more and more passengers boarded and
fewer and fewer of these were Indians. Once across
the Mississippi River, villages turned into towns, and
towns into cities.

Elizabeth, New Jersey, was a giant metropolis.
Several women met Susan and Marguerite at the
train station. They were members of a group that
paid for the girls' tuition to the Institute. Susan and
Marguerite were very polite and so they smiled and
graciously greeted their benefactors. But the two
sisters barely heard a word the women said during
the buggy ride to the school because the city was
such a dazzling wonder.

Horse-drawn trolleys rattled noisily over cobblestone streets; carriages of every size dashed about; buildings stood side by side, as tall as small mountains. Iron Eye must have known this feeling of awe and wonder when he traveled with his fur-trapper father to cities like St. Louis, thought Susan. One Woman also must have felt this way. They, too, must have stood wide-eyed when they saw the fantastic world which white people had created.

Susan had never seen so many white people. Once upon a time Indians had lived along the east coast but now there were hardly any left. Iron Eye had said, "Look ahead and you will see nothing but the white man." And that was certainly true here in the East.

At the Elizabeth Institute, Susan and Marguerite studied the "Three Rs – Reading, wRiting and aRithmatic," also called the "Common Branches." They took classes in philosophy, literature and physiology.

But more than this, Susan learned about the way white people lived. She observed every detail of their clothing – from their elegant kid gloves to the tiny eyelets in their tight-fitting shoes. Susan and Marguerite wore white people's dresses, which Indians called "citizens clothes."

People were kind to the Omaha sisters. Teachers and other students were nearly as excited as Susan and Marguerite when word arrived in 1880 that the Ponca had won their court battle and regained all of their Nebraska reservation land along the Niobrara River.

Even so, Susan and Marguerite were a curiosity in the non-Indian world of east coast America. Sometimes when the sisters went with school friends to a shop downtown or to a park, people stared at them. Children pointed.

"Maybe we're the first Indians they've ever seen," said Marguerite.

An Omaha child was taught never to stare at a stranger. But being stared at didn't embarrass the sisters. They giggled. Susan remembered a time at the agency school when she first saw a white woman with blond hair. Its color was golden and seemed to sparkle in the sun. Susan could barely keep from touching it. Susan understood curiosity.

One day the headmistress of the Elizabeth Institute came to Susan's classroom.

"I received a letter from your sister, Susette," she said. "She's in New York and plans to come to Elizabeth for a visit."

"Here?" Susan asked, barely able to contain her excitement. She often thought of her family, but she didn't realize how homesick she was until the headmistress said Susette's name. "When? Today?"

"No, not until Thursday," the headmistress said. "That'll give us plenty of time to plan a party."

Ten years earlier, Susette attended the Institute. Now she was the school's most celebrated graduate because of something that happened since Susan and Marguerite came east.

After the Ponca trial, Susette became a celebrity. Mr. Tibbles, the newspaper editor, arranged a speaking tour in an effort to fight for Indian rights. Susette, along with Tibbles, Chief Standing Bear, and Susan's older brother, Francis LaFlesche, set out on the cross-country tour. Standing Bear was to be the star, but his interpreter, Susette, ended up stealing the spotlight. People loved her. Newspapers everywhere — Chicago, Pittsburgh, Philadelphia, Boston, New York — praised her. They called her by her Omaha name, Bright Eyes. They said she was an "Indian Princess."

"That's silly," said Marguerite, when Susette arrived and the three sisters were alone. "Why do you let them call you 'Princess'? Indians don't have kings and queens and princesses."

Susan pointed at Marguerite's shoes. "And Indians don't wear pointed-toe, lace-up shoes, either."

"They most certainly do if they want to," said Marguerite, indignantly. "Indians can do whatever they want."

"And those hard-soled shoes are better than moccasins if you're going to walk around on Elizabeth's cobblestone streets, right?" added Susette.

"Right," said Susan.

"The newspapers may call me anything they like – Bright Eyes or Indian Princess. They may even call me the Duchess of New York," she said with a laugh. "People come to see a real live Indian chief and a chief's daughter. That's fine, because while they are seeing us, I can tell them about Indian rights. I can tell them about broken treaties and forced removal f r o m homelands. This way they can understand Indians, as well as *see* Indians."

Susan and Marguerite remained at the Elizabeth Institute for three years. They didn't have the money to go home on holidays, but they stayed at classmates' homes. Susan liked school. She even grew used to the hustle and bustle of life in Elizabeth. On the day she and her sister boarded the train for home, Susan wondered if she would ever see such wondrous sights again. But as the locomotive clattered and screeched toward the western horizon, she was suddenly overcome with a great longing to see the prairie.

⊰4⊱

Owning the Land

When Susan left the Indian reservation three years earlier, the Omaha feared the U.S. military would force them to move to the Indian Territory. But now the tribe was relieved by the latest news from Washington, D.C. A special bill passed Congress just two weeks before Susan and Marguerite arrived home. It granted each Omaha – man, woman and child – the right to own a piece of land.

Ownership of land was new for the Omaha. In the old days, they shared the land. The earth was not something to own – any more than a person could own the wind or the water. Traditionally, the tribe raised a few crops in a community garden. But their biggest source of food was buffalo. Each year before harvest, they left the tribal crops to follow and hunt buffalo. The meat represented the Indians' greatest source of food during the winter.

When Iron Eye was a young man, millions of buffalo roamed the prairie. In 1883, the year after Susan arrived home, a group of scientists traveled across the western frontier and could only find about 200 buffalo.

Along with the buffalo, the traditions of the Indians were also vanishing. Their language, songs, games and other customs were no longer being passed from one generation to the next. Some people feared that these traditions would be lost forever. They hoped to find some way to preserve the Indian customs. One of those people was Alice Fletcher.

While living in Washington, D.C., Alice heard Susette and Chief Standing Bear during their speaking tour. Susette's passionate appeal for the rights of

Indians persuaded Alice to travel to Nebraska. She was an ethnologist, a scientist who studies the origins and culture of the different races. She was deeply interested in learning about Native American tribes.

After hearing Susette, Alice wanted to learn about the Omaha tribe, to study its history and its way of living. In 1882, she moved to Nebraska. She knew that many Indians were suspicious of white people. So to win their trust, she decided to live like the Omaha. She ate Indian food and lived in a tent. After many months, she slowly built lasting friendships. Her first friends were members of the LaFlesche family.

During her talks with the Omaha, Fletcher came to understand that the Indians wanted to find a way to make a living and to be independent from the U.S. Indian Agency. Knowing what had happened to the Ponca, the Omaha wanted to insure that they could never be removed from their land by the government. Many Indians and sympathetic white people believed that such security would come only when Indians owned the land in the same way that white people owned land.

Fletcher had many friends in Washington D.C., and she persuaded them to help the Omaha. Consequently, a law was passed – the 1882 Severalty Act –

granting each member of the tribe his or her own
plot of farm land.

When Iron Eye picked up Susan and Marguerite
at the train depot, he talked about the new law. As
the buckboard bounced over the dirt road, he
proudly pointed out the little wooden houses that
now dotted the rolling hills of the reservation. Although most Indians still lived in tepees and earth
lodges, nearly 120 Omaha families had built new
wooden houses.

Susan's family had changed during the three years
she was gone from the reservation. Francis now
worked for the Bureau of Indian Affairs in Washington, D.C. Rosalie was married and had two baby
boys. Suzette had married Mr. Tibbles.

Iron Eye and One Woman were preparing to
move. Each member of the family received a land
allotment. Susan was glad that she and other mem-

bers of the family had allotments close to each other.

That summer Susan helped her family prepare for the move. At night when she tried to sleep, she lay awake thinking about what she might do now. With her own plot of land, maybe she should start farming, like Rosalie and her husband. Or maybe, like Marguerite, she should take a job teaching at the mission school.

Summer wore on, and Susan grew more and more frustrated about finding something she wanted to do. Then one day while visiting the school, Susan heard a commotion in the front yard of the mission.

Her brother, Francis, home for a visit, had just driven a wagon to the front steps. In the wagon was a cot. On the cot was the body of a white woman – Alice Fletcher.

Alice Fletcher became a life-long friend of the LaFlesche family. A famous ethnologist, she helped record and preserve Native American culture.

⧗5⧗

Highflyer,
the White Woman

Francis and another man carried the cot, on which Alice Fletcher lay, up to the second floor of the mission. Susan led the way through the hall and opened the door to the parlor. The men carefully set the cot down near the unlit stove. A crowd of school children gathered around the door to see the famous scientist.

Alice's hands, pale as the moon, were folded across her chest like a corpse in a coffin. Her soft, round face was the color of a gray stone.

"Mashahathe," the children whispered to each other. It was the name given to Fletcher by the Omaha. It meant an eagle circling in the sky. The English translation was Highflyer.

"Operit Mashahathe," they whispered in Omaha, even though it was against the rules to speak their native language in the mission school.

Translated it meant, "The Highflyer has come."

Francis held a finger over his mouth to quiet the children. "Come away," he said, and stepping into the hall, he closed the door.

Susan walked over to the cot and stared down at the woman. Because Alice had gained the respect of the tribe, the U.S. government had given her the job of overseeing the allotments of land to the Omaha. As always, she was determined to do her best for her Omaha friends. She lived and worked in her tent. Indians came to visit her and to tell her which piece of reservation land they wanted to own. Alice processed the papers to make sure their allotments were registered correctly.

Susan often saw the short, plump woman walking up and down the hills and along the creek beds, measuring out land for each Omaha. Rosalie and other friends took food to her and, when it rained, they tried to talk her into moving into their warm, dry homes. Alice would not. She had to live near the allotments, she said, so she could get the Indians their land as soon as possible – she was their Highflyer.

Susan leaned over the body. She was only inches away from the stony face when suddenly the woman's eyes opened.

Susan leaped back. "You're alive," she gasped.

The woman coughed violently and tried to sit up.

"Oh, no," said Susan, coming to the woman's side, "you mustn't get up." Though certainly not dead, the woman was obviously very sick. Susan picked up a pillow from a nearby chair and placed it under Alice's head. "Lie back," Susan said, gently lowering her to the pillow.

Francis walked into the room. "I think we've found you a nurse," he said to Alice, when he saw Susan. He carried a large carpetbag. "I brought your clothes and books," he said. "You'll have to stay here until you're better."

Francis explained that two days earlier Alice was caught in a thunderstorm. Though completely soaked, she continued to trudge across the fields, until she finally collapsed from exhaustion. When Francis found her, she could not walk and was in severe pain. The Indian Agent doctor said she had rheumatism. Alice needed plenty of bed rest and medical care.

Now Susan had something to occupy her time. She nursed Alice Fletcher.

"Susette says that you and Marguerite are Elizabeth Institute graduates," Fletcher said to Susan one day. Sitting up on her cot, Fletcher set down a large ledger full of the details about the Omaha allotments.

"Yes," Susan said, as she smoothed the sheet on Alice's cot. "All three of us went there."

"That's an extraordinary accomplishment for one Indian family."

"My father wants us all to go to school."

"Joseph is a very wise man," said Alice. "He and I talked about Hampton Institute. We're trying to make arrangements for your brother, Carey, to go there."

Hampton Institute was a school for boys in Virginia. Started after the Civil War, the school was created for black people, newly freed from slavery. In 1879, it opened its doors to Native Americans. Susan was glad for her brother's opportunity, but she was also envious.

"Where do girls go to school?" Susan asked Fletcher.

"Girls?" she asked. "Do you mean for higher education?"

Susan nodded. Alice frowned, as if pondering the questions.

"There're a few new ones, fairly good I'm told," she said. She picked up a pen and wrote something on the ledger. "Mount Holyoke, Smith, Vassar, and Wellesley," she said absently.

"Are they for white girls?" Susan asked. She said it so softly that she didn't think the woman heard.

Alice's hand stopped writing. "Yes, white," she said. "Are you wanting to go back to school?" But Susan didn't have to answer. Fletcher could see the eagerness on her face. "Why do you want to go to school?"

"Why did you want to go to Harvard?" Susan asked. She didn't mean to sound impertinent, but she believed that of all the people living on the reservation today, Alice Fletcher must surely be the one who could understand the appeal of going to school.

Alice laughed. The quick wit of Joseph LaFlesche's children amazed and delighted her. She had only intended to remain with the Omaha a few months, gather ethnological information and then move on to other tribes. But she had become irresistibly attached to these Nebraska Indians, especially to their leader's family. She had even asked Francis if he would like to co-author a book about the Omaha culture.

"Because I wanted to study ethnology," Alice answered. "Do you want to study that too?"

"I don't know. Maybe. I'm not sure what I want to

do. I just know I want to keep studying."

Nothing more was said about school for several weeks. Then one day when Susan came in to visit her patient, Alice pulled a sheet of paper out of a stack of letters. She handed the paper to Susan.

It was an application to Hampton Institute.

"It's not filled out," Susan said, puzzled by the blank lines. She and Marguerite had helped their brother complete the school's form. "I thought that Carey had already applied to Hampton."

"It isn't Carey's application," said Fletcher. "It's yours."

"Mine? But it's a boys' school." For an instant, Susan imagined that Alice was suggesting that she apply to Hampton and pretend to be a boy!

"Not any more," said Fletcher. "They've decided to admit girls."

Susan stared at Alice as if the woman were an unearthly magician. "You did it. Just like the Severalty Act. Do you know everyone in the United States?"

Fletcher laughed so hard she started coughing. Finally she said that Mr. Samuel Armstrong, head of the school, had been thinking about admitting girls for a long time. Alice's letter to him – along with supporting letters from many of her friends – was the encouragement he needed.

Susan tried to think of all the obstacles that might prevent her from going to Hampton. She wasn't worried about her grades from Elizabeth Institute. She did well in school. Money was certainly a concern, but Fletcher said she would help find scholarships. One obstacle arose, though, that Susan never imagined: Iron Eye.

When asked about Susan going to Hampton, her father's face darkened, reminding everyone why his Indian name was Iron Eye. He hit his fist against his chest for emphasis and spoke in French, which he did only when he was especially annoyed.

"Absolutement non!" he said.

This is Susan's mother, One Woman. Born to Nicomi, an Omaha-Oto-Iowa woman, and Dr. John Gale, an army doctor, One Woman was called Mary Gale by white people.

⊰6⊱

Iron Eye Thinks

In the Sacred Legend, the Omaha recorded the history of the tribe. It included ancient stories of struggle and of joy. The Legend encouraged the people to move ahead only after careful thought and study. Good things came from thoughtfulness; bad things came from thoughtlessness. Over and over, the Legend noted, "And the people thought."

When Iron Eye hit his chest and said, "Absolutement non," Alice Fletcher remained calm. For more than a year, she had studied the history and culture of the Omaha. She knew many things about the Sacred Legend. She said with a smile, "Will you think about it, Joseph?"

Sending young children away from home was very much against Indian tradition. Iron Eye broke with that tradition when he allowed his daughters to attend Elizabeth Institute. But even more radical was

41

letting boys and girls live near each other and sit together in the same classrooms. It was too shocking for some Indian parents to accept.

For several days Iron Eye remained silent on the subject of Hampton. Susan almost gave up hope. Then one day Iron Eye came to the mission and stood at the parlor door where Susan was tending to Alice, who was still recovering from rheumatism.

"I say yes to this boy-girl school," he said. And then he left.

Susan watched as her father walked across the yard and disappeared into the woods. His big shoulders seemed a little stooped, as if he carried a heavy burden.

Five years before Susan was born, Iron Eye asked the Omaha to send their children to the newly built Presbyterian mission school. The Indians didn't like that idea because they always taught their children at home. As an example Iron Eye sent his own children to the school. The first child to go was Iron Eye's oldest boy. One day word came that the boy was sick. Iron Eye and One Woman rushed to the school, but they were too late. The boy died. All night Iron Eye sat cradling the body of his son.

Even after that tragedy, Iron Eye continued to believe with all his heart that his children and all the Omaha must learn the new culture of white people. But the change from one culture to another was very hard for a man who grew up living and loving the Indian way of life. He had made many sacrifices to this new culture. Sending his daughters to Hampton was just one more.

As Susan watched her father disappear down the path, she made a promise to herself: From this day on she would dedicate her life to her people, just as Iron Eye had done.

This is a picture of Susan (standing) when she was about 14 years old. She was attending Hampton Institute then. Marguerite is on the right and two Omaha friends are on the left.

⚜7⚜

Hampton, Virginia

In 1884 Susan and Marguerite boarded a train again, this time for Hampton Normal and Agricultural Institute in Virginia. Other Omaha children went, too. Susan's sister, Lucy, and her husband, Noah, had already begun classes.

Hampton prepared its students for life on a farm. During the morning, African American and Native American boys and girls attended regular school classes. In the afternoon, they worked at very practical occupations. The boys worked in the fields. They learned about planting and harvesting. The girls practiced domestic skills: sewing, cooking, cleaning.

The man who started the school, Brigadier General Samuel Armstrong, believed that labor helped a person grow spiritually, mentally and physically. "We learn by doing," Armstrong said. Armstrong began the school with 15 students. By the time Susan enrolled there were several hundred.

Students at Hampton also learned to respect their classmates' diverse backgrounds. Black students and Indians from many tribes were taught mutual cooperation. A group of Hampton boys, called the Helping Hand Society, sent money to an Omaha family who lost their home during a tornado. Most of the Society's members were Sioux, the ancient enemy of the Omaha.

Each morning Susan woke up at five o'clock. She and the other girls put on their uniforms – dark dresses that buttoned up to the neck, and high-top shoes fastened by a long row of buttons.

Hampton's program was divided between two levels: one level for students who could speak English and the other level for students who couldn't. Susan and Marguerite were among the Indians who spoke the language very well. Often during the afternoon they tutored the non-English speaking students.

Not everything was hard work though. Two times

a month the boys and girls came together for a party. They played games, performed plays and musical programs.

Susan and Marguerite enjoyed the social life. In a few months, Marguerite fell in love with a student named Charles Felix Picotte. He was a Sioux.

Susan wrote home to Rosalie about the couple. "Mag and her Felix have a mutual admiration society. He says, 'Daisy [Marguerite's nickname] is so good to me; life could not be without her.' She says, 'Charles is so good to me. I don't think it would be possible to quarrel'."

Susan liked the company of several boys. She sent many letters home describing boys she met. In one letter, she wrote, "Sam is very nice…Walter is helping me learn to skate…The girls tease me unmercifully about Ashley."

One boy, however, particularly interested Susan. He was a Sioux named Thomas Ikinicapi. His friends called him T.I.

Even after attending four years at Hampton, T.I. spoke very little English. But he didn't need language to let Susan know that he cared about her very much. He always made a point of sitting beside her at weekend dinners. He walked with her after church. When Brig. Gen. Armstrong called, "Pick a partner," during one of the Saturday evening games,

This is Susan's sister, Rosalie LaFlesche Farley. She lived and worked on the reservation all her life. The mother of ten children, Rosalie played a vital role in helping her tribe make the often painful adjustment to a new way of living.

T.I. always made a dash for Susan. Sometimes other boys would ask her first, and a downcast T.I. would stand off to the side and watch.

Susan wrote home about T.I. He was gentle, she told Rosalie, and "*without exception* the handsomest Indian I ever saw."

Susan tried to teach him English, but without much luck. Despite his own trouble with getting good grades, T.I. was proud of Susan's achievements.

By her second year at Hampton, she was recognized as one of the school's best scholars. One day Miss Patterson, a favorite teacher, asked to speak to Susan privately.

"Gen. Armstrong and other staff members have been discussing your future," said Patterson. "We think it's highly likely that you could be accepted in college. Does that interest you?"

In her mind, Susan could see the smiling face of

48

her father. She imagined that he, too, was hearing this conversation – the daughter of Iron Eye accepted into a college!

"My father would be pleased," Susan said.

"It'll take determination and commitment," said Patterson. "You'll have to want to go very much."

Few Indians went to college and even fewer Indian girls. The problem wasn't only making good grades. Indian families simply didn't have the money to send their children to college.

"The problem is more than paying for college," Patterson said, as if she could read Susan's mind. "You'll need a clear vision of your future, and you can't be distracted by anything which could interfere with that future. If you want to go to college, you'll have to give up any ideas you have of getting married or having a family now."

Susan realized that Miss Patterson was talking about T.I. He was the distraction she was warning Susan to avoid. No one suggested that Marguerite should erase Charles Picotte from her future plans, and it was common knowledge that the two had talked about marriage. But then Marguerite wasn't a possible candidate for college.

"I've worried about how to discuss this with you," Miss Patterson said, when Susan didn't say anything. "Thomas is a goodhearted man, and it might be different if he had the abilities to go to college, too."

Like Susan, T.I. was trying to make the shift from the Indian world to the white world. Susan remembered Iron Eye and his unwavering dedication to insuring that his children would build a life in this new world. When T.I. was a little boy, no one urged him to go to school or encouraged him to speak English. T.I. had no one like Iron Eye.

"If you decide to go to college, we'll do everything possible to help you," said Patterson. "I'm hoping you'll give serious consideration to what I've said."

For several days, in the Omaha tradition, Susan thought hard about T.I. and about college and her future. Mostly she thought of Iron Eye. Yes, he wanted his children to build a life in the new world, but he also expected that they would build a bridge that would help other Omaha find that new world, too. Susan realized this when she came to Hampton. Now she realized that becoming the person her father wanted her to be would require sacrifice.

Iron Eye had never wavered from that sacrifice. Neither would Susan.

⋇8⋇

Salutatorian

While thinking about her future, Susan made an important decision: she would become a doctor. The idea first occurred to her during the weeks she nursed Alice Fletcher.

While living in Elizabeth, New Jersey, and Hampton, Virginia, Susan saw hospitals and wished that her own people had such fine facilities for health care. Although a doctor hired by the U.S. government worked at the Indian Agency, reservation Indians lacked good medical assistance. Dramatic changes in food, clothes and housing weakened the immunities of many of them. The Omaha and other Indians suffered and even died because they didn't receive proper care. Even young men like Charles Picotte and Thomas Ikinicapi were often sick.

Long before Susan was born, Iron Eye told the Omaha to give up their old tradition of living in

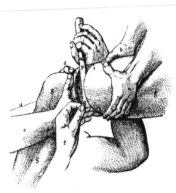

tepees and earth lodges. He taught them to build wooden houses. His home was the first wooden house in America built by an Indian. During its construction, he stepped on a nail. The wound became infected. Medical care was far away. Eventually Iron Eye's leg was amputated. For 26 years he had walked with a wooden leg.

By working as a doctor Susan could help solve some of these widespread and debilitating health problems. Medicine was a way she could serve her people and make her father proud. But first she had to get into medical school.

True to Miss Patterson's promise, the staff at Hampton did everything they could to help. When Susan picked the Woman's Medical College of Pennsylvania as the school she wanted to attend, Brig. Gen. Armstrong wrote a glowing recommendation, "I regard her as about the finest, strongest Indian character we have had at this school. She is level-headed, earnest, capable…, quite equal to medical studies…She is independent, naturally a deep but not a sentimental woman."

The school doctor, Martha M. Waldron, who had attended the Woman's Medical College, also wrote a letter on Susan's behalf. Both Dr. Waldron and Alice Fletcher set out to find a scholarship for Susan. Fletcher knew the president of the Connecticut Indian Association, a group dedicated to helping Native Americans. The group agreed to pay for part of Susan's college expenses.

Meanwhile, graduation day at Hampton was fast approaching. With her life at Hampton coming to an end, Susan's future was still uncertain. The Medical College hadn't accepted or rejected her application.

Just a few days before commencement, Susan received a stack of mail. It appeared to be her usual letters from home and from friends in Elizabeth, New Jersey, but in the stack was a crisp white envelope with her name and address written in formal, fancy script. The return address was Philadelphia, Pennsylvania. Susan's friends gathered around as she carefully tore the seal and unfolded the letter. A great whoop went up when she read, "We are pleased to inform you...."

"I'm accepted!" she shouted, waving the letter overhead. And certainly that was wonderful news. But even as she celebrated, Susan realized that acceptance was only the first hurdle. Unless she could

This is Susan's graduation class at Hampton Institute. She is sitting, second from the left. Charles Picotte, Marguerite's future husband is standing at the far left. Susan's sister, Lucy, is standing, the last person on the right.

find the money – *all* the money – she wouldn't be going to Philadelphia and she wouldn't become a doctor.

However, more good news soon followed. The Hampton faculty chose Susan as the graduating class's salutatorian. That honor meant that she would deliver the opening speech at commencement.

On graduation day, May 20, 1886, Susan sat on the stage with other honored guests. After being introduced, she stepped to the podium and looked out over an audience larger than the entire Omaha tribe. Besides her classmates, there were more than 1,000 guests. Alice Fletcher was among them.

Susan's speech was titled, "My Childhood and Womanhood." She talked about her life growing up as an Omaha Indian girl. She talked about her large family and the joys they shared. But times have changed, she told the audience. "We have to prepare our people to live in the white man's way, to use the white man's books, and his laws." But it took many years for white people to write those books and laws and to build their way of life, she pointed out. The Indians were just beginning this new journey. It would take time. She asked her audience to be patient.

When she finished, one of the guests of honor, Gen. Byron Cutcheon, a Civil War Medal of Honor winner, presented Susan with a gold medal. It was given to the student with the highest examination score.

The General said, "This is for the excellence with which you have laid a foundation… It is a great thing to be one of the first women of your race to lay this foundation…. I charge you to regard it as your duty to live for your people. To devote yourself to them."

An area newspaper later reported that after the

presentation "thundering applause" rose from the audience.

Friends stopped Susan as she left the stage. They asked her what she thought when she heard the General's praise and the applause. She didn't really hear anything, she said – it was all "as in a dream."

The day after graduation, the Connecticut Indian Association agreed to pay Susan's *entire* costs at the medical school.

The dream was just beginning.

✳9✳

Live Bodies
and Dead Bodies

Susan looked at the list of subjects for her
first year of medical school: chemistry, physiology, histology, *materia medica* [drugs and medi-
cines], general therapeutics, obstetrics and anatomy.
The names sounded impressive – a Hampton friend
said the names sounded a little scary – but Susan
could hardly wait to start her classes.

Only chemistry caused her any concern. Just to
make sure she understood everything that the instructor talked about in the lecture, Susan reviewed
the information with a friend, a second-year student.
It was a good thing Susan worked so conscientiously
because, in order to pass, students had to make at
least 90 percent on all their tests.

Everyday Susan learned something new about
health care. She often wrote home, offering medical
advice to the family. When her mother had a sore on

her hand, Susan sent home an antiseptic medicine and castile soap. She ordered her father a new and better fitting artificial leg. When Rosalie's husband, Ed Farley, became sick, Susan wrote, "Tell him 'Dr.' Sue orders less quinine and more time for his meals." When Rosalie was pregnant, Susan told her sister not to lift heavy things and to get plenty of fresh air and sleep. "Stop worrying," Susan advised, "and take more time to read and tell stories to the children."

One of her funniest letters home described something that happened the first time her class observed an operation at the Woman's Clinic. The students from Jefferson Medical School, a men's college, came to observe the operation, too.

Very few women were doctors at this time. Even women who received medical degrees weren't allowed to practice in many hospitals. Consequently, people often had the false impression that women lacked the mental and physical strength to do medical work. That's what students from Jefferson Medical School thought.

When the students came into the surgery room, the men took the front seats closest to the patient. They didn't even bother to look back at the women students behind them. One of the men made a comment about "the girls screaming and fainting" when the patient's body was cut open. The other men laughed.

As the instructor pulled back the sheet covering the patient, Susan and the other girls leaned forward to get a better look. Susan watched the scalpel slice slowly across the skin. A thin red line of blood rose up from the flesh. In the next instant, a loud thud was heard. One of the Jefferson men toppled forward in a faint. He had to be carried from the operating room.

Susan and the other women laughed about the "wilting violets" from Jefferson for many days afterwards. Susan wrote home, "I wasn't even thinking of fainting" and neither were any "of the girls."

Susan even enjoyed her anatomy class and dissecting cadavers – dead bodies. She gaily informed Rosalie that she was "going to wield the knife tonight – not the scalping knife though." In her letters she described every detail of the dissection. The class met after dinner. The cadavers were kept in tubs of formaldehyde, a  liquid used to preserve the bodies. The strong smell of the liquid filled the room. Even though the women students wore long, thick aprons, the chemical odor clung to their clothes after they left class.

Six girls worked on each cadaver. Using sharp knives, they first cut through the cold, gray skin. They then peeled back the thin tissue covering the muscles. Next, muscles were carefully cut apart in order to study the blood vessels and nerves embedded inside. Finally the skeleton was revealed and each bone was carefully examined.

"It is interesting to get all the arteries and their branches," Susan wrote back home. "Everything has a name, even the little tiny holes in the bones. It is splen- did."

The more she learned about medicine and good health habits, the more she realized how far her Omaha people were from liv- ing healthy lives. The Omaha needed proper medicine, a well-equipped hos- pital and a dedi- cated doctor who knew them and spoke their lan- guage. Susan hoped to fill those needs when "Dr. Sue" returned to the reservation.

⇥ 10 ⇤

The Dollar Bill

While attending school in Elizabeth and Hampton, Susan lived in dormitories with other girls. Closely supervised, these living quarters were on the school campuses. By contrast, in Philadelphia, known as the City of Brotherly Love, she lived in a boarding house, along with many students and business people who worked in the city.

From the first day Susan walked into her room in Philadelphia, she was homesick. She wrote a letter home saying, "Three years from now will be Paradise when we can all be together." Most of the time, though, she found a happy distraction in her classes and school friends.

Most Native Americans only knew white culture from the people who lived and traveled through the west. Susan's experience was much different. Her boarding house was right in the middle of a huge east coast metropolis. Every day she had the chance to see the city's diverse immigrant population, both rich and poor. She strolled with friends through magnificent parks and along wide boulevards; she visited art museums and historical landmarks; she attended the theater and musical concerts.

Like many women students at the medical school, Susan's roommate came from a well-to-do family. Susan often visited the homes of these wealthy school friends. Describing to her family one such visit, she wrote:

I had a great big bedroom to myself, with an ivory comb and brush. Then at breakfast, the first course was oranges and we had finger bowls. They just dip in their fingers and wipe them on napkins. Then all was re- *moved and we had kidney and gravy, potatoes and bread and butter and coffee. The coffee was in a great big silver urn and had a flame under it and Mrs. Ogden turned on a faucet and hot coffee came out.*

By comparison on the reservation, large families lived together in two to four rooms in small wooden houses. In the old days, the Omaha built their tepees and earth lodges next to rivers and creeks. Now they lived on farms and often traveled long distances to carry water from a spring or well. Though the houses looked like white people's houses on the outside, inside they often had no rugs or dishes and few pieces of furniture. These things were too expensive. White people also wore clothes that were expensive and elaborate.

One day Susan and her roommate went together to a reception at the school. Susan wore a dress given to her by the ladies at the Connecticut Indian Association. Susan was always grateful for the clothes and supplies purchased by the ladies. She called them her "many mothers" and often wrote them notes of thanks. At the reception Susan wore "a pretty blue [dress] made of a sort of flannel with ruching at the neck and sleeves," she wrote to Rosalie. Her roommate wore an elegant black silk and lace dress and kid gloves.

Kid gloves were very fashionable. Susan wanted a pair. When one of her lady benefactors gave her one dollar for spending money, Susan folded the money neatly inside her little purse. What color gloves should she buy? Black? White? Or maybe a soft brown, the color of one of the fawns she often saw in the hills back home in Nebraska. And then, while walking across the park to the glove-makers' shop, Susan saw a small boy carrying a little wooden horse.

She looked down at her purse. She could feel the outline of the folded dollar. Returning to the boarding house, Susan slipped the bill inside her steamer trunk. The holidays were near. She would save the money to buy gifts for Rosalie's children.

A short time later, Rosalie sent Susan a letter. One Woman, their mother, was very ill. Other Indians in the tribe became sick during that autumn. For many months, food and money were scarce. Rosalie said that the family was worried that Susan, too, might be suffering.

Susan wrote reassuringly to Rosalie. "Tell Father and Mother my boarding house is fine," she said. "I have such good things to eat. I am never hungry here."

Then she dug through her trunk and pulled out the dollar bill. She put it in the envelope with a little note to Rosalie: "Buy meat for Mother, maybe chicken."

⇥ 11 ⇤

Terrible News

Iron Eye and One Woman were growing old. Susan missed them. Knowing the hardships of living on the reservation, she worried about them, too. She hadn't been home in several years, but after two years in medical school, she returned to the reservation for summer vacation.

That summer, although Iron Eye did not feel very strong, he helped Alice Fletcher and Francis research the ancient customs of the Omaha. There was only one man left in the tribe who knew the words for one of the tribe's oldest ceremonies. His name was Yellow Smoke, and he was very old. He didn't want to tell the secret words to an outsider like Alice.

Francis asked Iron Eye to help convince Yellow Smoke to tell the words to the researchers. At first Iron Eye said no. Perhaps it was better that the old ways die, he said, that the secret ceremonies sink into the earth and vanish like dust over the prairie. But Iron Eye promised that he would think about it.

One day in the late summer Iron Eye asked Susan to go with him to Yellow Smoke's farm. The old man still lived much of the time in a tepee, and he still spoke in the old language. Yellow Smoke invited his friend inside the tepee, and the two men sat around the circle of fire stones in the center. For a long time they sat together and said nothing. After a while, Iron Eye stood up and joined Susan who had remained in the wagon. The two drove back home.

A few days later, Iron Eye again asked Susan to go with him to Yellow Smoke's farm. Once more the

two old men sat around the fire stones. They spoke a few words about the good harvest, but mostly they sat in silence.

Several other times that summer Susan drove her father to Yellow Smoke's farm. Sometimes the men talked about old friends or about long-ago buffalo hunts or about Washington, D.C. (both men had visited the capital on behalf of the tribe). But mostly they sat quietly.

Then one day Yellow Smoke said, "If I tell Highflyer about our grandfathers' secret words, their spirits will be angry."

"Then they will be angry with me, not you," said Iron Eye. "For I say it is good to put away the past in this way and cross over to the future."

Yellow Smoke said he would think hard on this. And one day he invited Iron Eye, Francis and Alice Fletcher to sit around the tepee fire stones with him. There he began to tell the old, old Omaha story. Francis and Alice took many pages of notes. They asked Yellow Smoke questions and carefully recorded every detail – every dance step, song, chant, costume – of the ceremony. Francis and Alice also talked to many other elderly Omaha. And so the ancient Omaha culture and history did not vanish like dust on the prairie, but it lived forever in the book called *The Omaha Tribe*.

That summer Susan not only drove her father to and from Yellow Smoke's farm, she also did all the major chores on the LaFlesche farm because One Woman was still sick. Susan cooked, sewed, stored the hay, and staked out a new fence.

A measles epidemic raged through the reservation during the early summer, and so Susan also visited sick Omaha families, each day traveling 25 miles in the wagon.

In a letter to a friend back east, Susan wrote, "I can tell you one thing, and that is that a western woman has to know how to do everything that a man does, besides her own work, for she has to be ready for any emergency."

Susan returned to school in the fall. She had given her mother and father a list of foods they should eat and other advice about how to stay healthy and strong. But she still worried about them. She only had one more year before graduation. When she returned to the reservation then, she would be able to look after them all the time.

Even during the train trip back east, Susan began to think about the final exam next spring. If she could just make it past that last big hurdle, she would graduate. She knew how proud her father would be at her graduation, sitting in the audience watching his daughter receive a medical degree.

Susan had just settled into the routine of classes in Philadelphia when she received terrible news from home. Iron Eye was dead.

12

Doctor Wisdom

Shortly after Susan left the reservation for Philadelphia, Iron Eye became feverish and died within a few days.

For many weeks after his death, Susan went about her daily business – attending classes, visiting friends, going to church. Although her body moved through these activities, her mind floated off somewhere else. She thought about her father. She could hear his gentle voice asking her to do something and then adding, "It will please me." All her life, she had worked to please him.

When he learned of her desire to go to medical school, he had said, "Daughter, I will tell you what you might do as a doctor. Learn all they can teach you in that city of brotherly love and say, 'I owe this doctor wisdom to the Omaha.' And then come

69

home. Do this and it will please me."

Susan studied hard. As always, she worried about examinations. "I feel as if I don't know a single thing," she wrote a friend, "and my degree is only six weeks off – at least I hope it is."

But Susan didn't have to worry because, once again, graduation day brought her honors. On March 14, 1889, she graduated at the top of her class of 36 women. Unlike Susan, most of her classmates had university degrees, in addition to their medical schooling. The commencement speaker recognized Susan's great achievement, "She will stand among her people as the first woman physician. Surely we may record with joy such courage, constancy and ability."

Susan did so well on her exams that she was selected as one of six women to intern for four months at Philadelphia's Woman's Hospital. Before she finished her internship and returned to Nebraska, Susan traveled around New England speaking to her "Connecticut mothers," as she called the women who had paid for her medical school.

Now her years in the east came to a close. Susan had spent most of her teenage life living and going to school away from home. Hard work and perseverance paid off. The dream had come true. She was a doctor.

The train rumbled toward the west – through the

Appalachian Mountains, across the Mississippi River, over the Missouri River. Dr. Susan LaFlesche was going home, taking the "doctor wisdom" back to her people.

⇥ 13 ⇤

Doctoring Her People

Much had changed on the reservation
while Susan was away. Susette and Thomas
Tibbles now lived in the city of Omaha. Rosalie and
Ed Farley had several children. Marguerite, who
married Charles Picotte, taught at the agency school.
After Iron Eye's death, Charles took over farming the
LaFlesche land. The family soon grew to love this
kind and hardworking Sioux. Lucy and Noah also
were farming their allotment.

In 1887, Congress passed a law, the Dawes Severalty Act [also called the General Allotment Act].
The Act granted other Indian tribes the same land
allotments that had been granted several years earlier to the Omaha. The law divided most Indian
reservations into individual plots of land. No longer
would each tribe own its reservation communally.
Now each tribe member would own his or her own

separate tract of land (40 to 160 acres).

For members of the Omaha who accepted allotments, the new law granted them U.S. citizenship. This right wasn't granted to other Indians until 1924. With citizenship, the Omaha could vote and were expected to obey the same laws and regulations as other citizens. Susette and her husband had worked very hard to get the law passed. However, other members of the LaFlesche family weren't so sure that the law would solve the Omaha's problems. Susan, for one, could see that citizenship would not change the health habits of the tribe or make adjusting to a new culture any easier.

Susan's first job as a doctor was in the government's agency school in Macy, Nebraska. But soon the government put her in charge of the entire Omaha tribe, 1,244 members. Previously, the doctors hired by the government couldn't speak the Omaha language. This made getting good health care very difficult for the Indians who were still struggling with English. However, with Susan, the tribe had a doctor they could talk to.

Susan set up an office in the agency schoolhouse. To encourage reluctant Indians to come for a doctor's examination, she decorated her office with plants, pictures and comfortable chairs. She had games and books for the children. Because money was scarce on the reservation, most of her patients paid for her services with vegetables and fruits from their gardens.

Pretty soon Susan's office was full of children and their families. When the weather was bad, old Omaha men and women often gathered in her office where it was warm and friendly. Often people came to see her for reasons other than health care. They wanted advice about business or the law or even personal matters. They trusted and respected her opinion.

Frequently Susan's patients were too weak to come to her office, so she visited them in their homes. She never turned down a request. Sometimes in the middle of the night, someone would knock on her front door. A parent might come to beg for help for a feverish child. Or a frightened child might arrive, asking for help for a parent. "Please come to my house. My mother cannot move her leg."

Walking or riding her horse, Susan traveled all over the reservation, attending to the sick. In sunny or freezing weather, Susan would pack her doctor's bag and start out at seven in the morning to make her rounds. Often she didn't return home until 10:00 o'clock at night. Traveling was difficult, over dirt roads and grassy paths. Remembering those long, hard journeys Susan later said, "After trying for some time to go about on horseback, I broke so many bottles and thermometers that I had to give that up." She finally bought a buggy to make traveling smoother.

Several generations of a single Omaha family often lived in the same small house. This caused diseases to spread very quickly. Unsanitary conditions also allowed diseases to spread. Susan was constantly treating people for ailments like influenza, dysentery, cholera, tuberculosis (TB) and conjunctivitis (an eye disease). She wrote in one of her annual government reports, "Tuberculosis of the lungs seems to be on the increase in our tribe. In place of wild game, diseased meat is eaten in many cases and much pork. In place of the airy tent, [we have] houses where often in one room two families are found with doors and windows closed night and day, so we cannot wonder that scrofula is the result."

Late one night Susan was awakened by a loud clatter. At first she thought it was the winter wind howling around the house, but she soon discovered a woman was pounding on the front door.

"My daughter cannot get air," said the woman. "Please come."

Susan recognized the woman and knew about her daughter. She was a young girl who recently attended Hampton Institute but who had to return home because she had tuberculosis.

Susan gathered medicines and equipment into her black doctor bag. Very early that morning, she started for the girl's house. It was 20° below zero. Under a sky the color of steel, the frozen ground crunched like broken glass beneath the carriage wheels.

The family lived in a one-room house. In a dark corner, the sick girl lay on a bed heaped with buffalo robes and makeshift covers.

"We keep her warm," said the mother, crying softly.

"She will grow well now," her father said, confidently. He pointed to Susan's bag. "The medicine doctor will find a healing potion in that box."

But hearing the raspy breaths coming from the poor girl, Susan wasn't sure there was much she could do. All around the bed were the girl's favorite reminders of life at Hampton. There were books with ivy leaves pressed between the pages. There were copies of the *Southern Workman*, the school's newspaper. Mostly there were photographs of smiling friends.

77

Later Susan would write about the visit. "The girl and everything in her quarter of the room were clean and neat as could be." The girl had learned that neatness while living at Hampton, Susan surmised. The rest of the room was almost bare. Dark rags covered the two windows. Clothes hung on pegs. A few dirty dishes and a hollowed-out gourd, which served as a common drinking cup, sat on an old table. Susan could not see any food in the house.

"How long since you've eaten?" Susan asked the family.

The father answered, "Not so many crops this year. But I hunt for rabbit – for her." He pointed to his daughter.

This was what Susan suspected. The family had little food and what they had went to the sick girl.

"Bad cough?" said the mother, as if pleading with Susan to say that her daughter suffered only a mild and curable ailment.

But Susan didn't believe the girl would live through the day. The cough was, indeed, deep and harsh. Its violent outbreaks shook her frail body like a convulsion. Susan realized that the influenza had only made the tuberculosis worse.

Susan took some medicine out of her bag. "This will help with the cough," she said. "I'll be back before dark. Bring water to the house before I return."

Susan made her other house calls that day. Late in the afternoon she returned home and packed a sled – for it had begun to snow – full of food. Along with Marguerite and another teacher at the school, Susan returned to the tubercular girl's house.

The girl lived for two more weeks. In that time, Susan came at least once a day. She did what she could to comfort the dying girl. Sometimes Susan spent the night. She also cooked for the family and showed them how to keep their food-serving areas clean. She brought them several drinking cups. "Never drink from the same cup," she told them.

All that winter and spring, the desperate appeals for medical help continued from other families. In the next few years, Susan saw hundreds of patients. She visited everyone who called for her help. But after four years of constant work, Susan had to stop.

Dr. Susan LaFlesche Picotte, on the left, is sitting with her sons, Caryl and Pierre, and her mother, One Woman.

⇥ 14 ⇤

In Sickness and In Health

Susan's family also suffered from the out breaks of disease which swept through the Omaha community. After months of illness, Charlie Picotte, Marguerite's husband, died in 1892. Like many Indians, he tried hard to make the shift from the old ways to the new. Charlie was a tall and vigorous man, but the enormous changes in diet and living conditions were too much for him. A few weeks before his death, he wrote a letter to Hampton Institute. He thanked his teachers and friends for their help and guidance. He said he was sorry that he could not continue to work as an example for his people.

Shortly after Charlie's death, Susan learned that her friend from Hampton, Thomas Ikinicapi, had also died. T.I., too, had tried unsuccessfully to adjust to the white culture.

Some people – Indians and non-Indians alike – believed that the Dawes Severalty Act would solve many of the Indians' problems. They hoped the change from communal ownership to private ownership would help the Indians become self-supporting. But this is not what happened. In fact, the new law made it easier for white people to settle on reservation land and to claim it as their own. In 1887 there were 138 million acres of Indian reservation land in the United States. By 1934, there were only 48 million acres belonging to the Indians.

The shrinking Indian land and the widespread health problems on the reservations caused many Native Americans to turn to a religious ceremony called Ghost Dancing. Ghost Dancers believed that the ceremony would summon up special powers.

They felt that by performing the Ghost Dance the buffalo would reappear and their old way of life would return.

The U.S. government, however, feared the ceremony would lead to war. So Congress passed a law banning the practice. In 1890 the government accused a tribe of Sioux of disobeying the law and ordered the U.S. military to stop the offenders. On December 29, the U.S. Seventh Cavalry rode onto the Pine Ridge Reservation and killed more than 250 men, women and children at a place called Wounded Knee Creek. Susan's sister Susette went to South Dakota to help care for the wounded.

During all these turbulent events, Susan struggled to make life better for the Omaha. But the long hours traveling through the wind and cold finally took their toll. Susan became sick. Her ears hurt and her head ached. She might have continued with her exhausting schedule even with the pain but there was someone else to consider. One Woman had become very ill, too. And so in October, 1893, Susan quit her job as government doctor.

Everyone was saddened about her resignation, but most people weren't surprised. The *Southern Workman*, Hampton Institute's newspaper, reported, "Dr. Susan LaFlesche, who has been doctor to the whole Omaha tribe for nearly five years – doing more than three strong men ought to do – finally had to resign."

But the next year Susan did something that surprised everyone. She married Henry Picotte. Henry had come to the funeral of his brother, Charles. No one knows for sure why or when Susan decided to marry. She always said that she would never marry – "I shall be the dear little old maid," she wrote Rosalie while in medical school. But one day in 1894, she announced that she and Henry were to be husband and wife.

Henry worked as a performer in a Wild West show. These traveling productions, such as the famous one starring Buffalo Bill Cody, attracted many Indians Henry's age. It was hard for young Indians to stay confined to the reservation. These young men could remember the excitement of the old days – hunting buffalo and roaming freely across the prairie. The glamorous Wild West shows let them relive, even if by pretending, those early experiences.

Susan's friends and family wondered why Susan, a doctor, would choose to marry a Wild West performer. Susan admitted that Henry was "utterly unlike" herself. Maybe the death of T.I. reminded her of the value of a loving relationship. Maybe the years of hard work doctoring other people's children made her wish she had her own family. And maybe it was simply that she loved Henry Picotte very much.

He was, as her family observed, a likeable and friendly man. And in the next few years, when he and Susan became parents of two boys, Susan wrote friends, "Henry worships the baby. They are the greatest of friends." The Picottes were a happy family. Henry and Susan's two boys – Caryl and Pierre – brought them great joy.

The family, including One Woman, moved into a house in Bancroft, Nebraska, which was on the south edge of the Omaha reservation. They planted an orchard and landscaped the yard with wonderful flowering bushes.

Susan's health gradually improved, and she resumed her medical practice. Henry tended the babies and worked at farming the LaFlesche allotments as his brother had done.

Susan opened her doctor's office to everyone, doctoring both white settlers and Indians. Once again she was on call 24 hours a day. In order for her patients to find her house at night, she left a lantern burning in the window.

One rainy night a young boy came looking for that light. The Bancroft telegraph operator had just received an urgent message that a woman at a nearby farm was having trouble in childbirth. Two doctors, who were already attending the woman, had sent the telegram. "Bring Dr. Picotte – quick."

The boy raced to the Picotte house. Susan was up and out the door in a flash. She and the boy rode through the storm, oftentimes having to follow the fence rows to find their way. All three doctors worked through the night. Later one of the doctors reported that the mother and baby had survived the night and were doing well, "thanks to the skill of Dr. Susan."

Besides administering to individual patients, Susan began dedicating much of her time to community health concerns. The greatest of these was alcoholism. When Iron Eye was alive, the tribe was free of problems with alcohol. Unfortunately, by the 1890s, drunkenness was a major problem among the Indians. A worried and angry Susan wrote an annual report to the Commissioner of Indian Affairs about

conditions on the reservation.

"Men and women died from alcoholism," she said, "and little children were seen reeling on the streets of the town. Drunken brawls in which men were killed occurred and no person's life was considered safe."

Congressional committees investigating problems on the reservations frequently sought Susan's testimony. When the courts reviewed crimes involving Indians, judges and lawyers often asked for her expert opinion on alcohol use among Indians.

There were dozens of tragic incidents that illustrated the problems. Susan told the story about the old Indian who was murdered by a young drunken Indian who then killed himself. She told another story of an Indian who fell from his horse and wasn't missed by his drunken friends until the next morning. By then he had frozen to death. She pointed out that Omaha families were being torn apart by alcoholism. If the problems weren't solved, Susan was afraid that alcoholism would continue from one generation to the next.

The Omaha were trying to think of themselves as American citizens. But it was hard. They missed the communal life of the tribe. They missed not having a strong leader who lived among them. They wanted to learn to farm but often lacked enough money to buy proper farming equipment. For some Indians drinking became a way to escape their problems.

Susan wanted her people to take responsibility for their own lives, but she realized that sometimes white people made that difficult. Some white people used alcohol to bribe Indians to sign over their lands and property. They used alcohol to buy Indians' votes during elections.

Susan fought to ban alcohol. She pleaded with the Indian Commissioner to stop the flow of liquor onto the reservation. After many years of testifying in Washington, writing angry letters and pleading with officials, Susan rejoiced when the U.S. Interior Department announced that liquor could not be sold in any town once part of the Omaha reservation.

It was a victory. But for one person the victory came too late. Susan's own husband, Henry Picotte, battled alcoholism for several years. In 1905 he died. Her friends and family rallied to her support with love and sympathy.

"There are times," she said to one friend, "when I get so lonely and want to see him so much." But Susan could not look backward. She had two little boys, seven and nine years old. And she had her mother, now almost 80. Together they would make a new life.

⊰ 15 ⊱

A Leader to Her People

Shortly after Henry's death, Susan moved her little family to Macy, the location of the Omaha Agency, where she continued her medical work. She also took on another job. The Presbyterian Church appointed her as missionary to her tribe. Susan was the first Indian ever given that role.

In the months to come, more and more Indians came to Susan for their spiritual, as well as medical help. One newspaper wrote that Susan offered "not only spiritual and medical advice but sympathy and the help of one Indian to her own people."

Susan's home in Macy was small. And so in 1906, she bought a plot of land in the new town of Walthill. Marguerite and her new husband, Walter Diddock, bought land across the street. Both Susan and the Diddocks built fine, big houses. Before long, nieces and nephews, aunts and uncles were visiting back and forth daily. Susan's sons thrived in the atmosphere of their large, energetic LaFlesche family. It reminded Susan of tribal life, when extended families were at the heart of existence.

Every Sunday, Uncle Walter would cook a big breakfast for everyone. He always made pancakes, the children's favorite. Susan – the family called her Dr. Sue – would walk into the Diddock kitchen and sniff.

She'd wrinkle her nose, as if she smelled something very unpleasant.

"Walter, why are you making those doughy cakes?" she'd say, sounding very stern. "Don't you know they'll lie in your stomach like leather?"

Uncle Walter would smile and go on flipping pancakes.

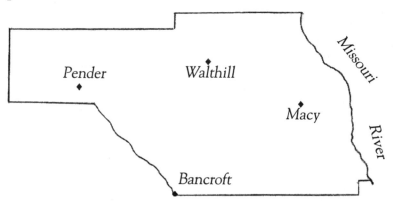

This is the Omaha Reservation. It is an enlargement of the shaded portion of the map on page 15.

And then she would sit down at the table between the children and spread a napkin across her lap. "So fry up two or three for me!" she'd say with a wink.

Susan's good humor made her popular among her patients as well as among her fellow doctors. She helped start the Medical Association of Thurston County and was a member of the Nebraska State Medical Society. She also served as Chairman of Public Health for the Nebraska State Federation.

Susan used her role in these organizations to continue to promote important health care matters. Several times during her medical practice she was called on to treat terrible diseases that became epidemics, fast spreading illnesses. Diphtheria, influenza, smallpox, tuberculosis – when these diseases struck the community, they spread from household to household like a prairie fire. No one was safe. Babies, old people, Indians and white people all suffered.

No vaccines existed in those days to immunize people against these scourges. Susan knew the answer was prevention, and the best prevention was sanitation.

During those days people used common drinking cups. Even in public places, when a person wanted a drink of water he or she would share the cup with everyone else. This spread germs. And so Susan started a statewide campaign to create laws against using a common cup. Within a few years, laws were passed to abolish the unhealthy practice. Sanitary drinking fountains were installed in schools. Soda fountains at drug stores used disposable paper cups to serve drinks and wooden spoons to serve ice cream.

Susan also organized an effort to educate people about the dangers of the housefly. She created a poster warning people to keep flies out of their homes and off their food. Mesh screens on doors and windows will protect a house, she said. Sprinkling lime or kerosene on a fly's favorite nesting place will stop the pest from breeding. Soon hardware stores were selling rolls of screen and flytraps.

People trusted Susan. They looked to her for spiritual and medical guidance. They also called on her when they needed a strong political voice in Washington, D.C.

Years earlier when the Indians received their allotments, the government made certain restrictions on the Indians' rights to use the money promised to them when they gave up their land to the U.S. The money was put "in trust."

This meant that, although the money belonged to the Indians, the government controlled it. The trust period was supposed to last for 25 years – until 1910. But as 1910 drew near, the government decided the Indians weren't yet ready to manage their own affairs. The trust would be extended for another 10 years.

This made Susan very angry. In an article for a newspaper in the city of Omaha, she explained the Indians' viewpoint.

We have rules and regulations to the right of us…to the left of us…behind us; do you wonder we object to the continuation of them in front of us?…Indians can trade at certain stores up to a certain amount. The superintendent inspects the bill and then if the department [in Washington] approves the number and size of prunes and the color of bananas, the government pays the bill out of the Indians' own money…One woman who had tuberculosis asked for her share [of trust funds]; it was badly needed. The Superintendent asked for it to be a 'special'…an order came for her to sign certain blanks; the Superintendent wrote that it was for immediate necessities…[the government] sent a new form to be signed. In the meantime she had died and was buried.

All the Omaha rose up against the trust extension. For the first time in many years they came together. Through the years the tribe had slowly pulled apart. Long gone were the days of tepees in a circle around a campfire. Now each family lived a separate life from other Omaha families. But in 1910 the proposed trust extension united them.

"No concessions!" they shouted at the meetings.

Many of their white neighbors supported them. One Nebraskan said that he was surprised the Indians had managed to survive the quarter of a century of allotment restrictions. He said that such restrictions "would have utterly ruined the same number of white people."

Many newspapers around the state spoke up for the Omaha. The editor of the *Walthill Times* wrote that the trust was "an unwise system of government supervision…every business action of the individual is supervised and hedged about with red tape."

The Omaha decided to send a delegation to Washington, D.C. The tribe unanimously chose Susan as one of the delegates.

Unfortunately, One Woman had recently died. She had been very sick for a long time. Susan, too, was ill. The headaches and earaches returned. She even lost much of her hearing. On top of everything else, she was battling a diphtheria epidemic.

When Susan said she didn't believe she could go

to Washington, the Omaha people said they wouldn't take no for an answer. They would come to her house, they said, and bodily put her on the train.

So Susan agreed to go. In early 1910, the Omaha delegation left for Washington. On February 7, Susan spoke before the Secretary of the Interior. She explained that many Indians had already died, never receiving their rightful share of the trust funds.

"I have several cases waiting for surgical operation," she said, "and the people want to use these moneys for expenses. Every day I receive letters imploring my help."

Within a month the government acted. The Secretary of Interior agreed to allow most of the Omaha to receive their rightful allotments immediately.

Back home in Nebraska, there was jubilation. The *Fremont Tribune* wrote, "Omahas won a triumph...[The] delegation was the wisest of the tribe, headed by a woman, a college graduate and skilled in medicine...Dr. Picotte drew up a second declaration of independence" for her people.

On the train bound for home, Susan thought about her father. Iron Eye had said that it was good to put away the past and cross over to the future. Maybe, at long last, the future had come for the Omaha.

This is the home built by Dr. Susan LaFlesche
Picotte in Walthill, Nebraska. It was one of the first
houses built in the town. Susan's sister, Marguerite and
her family, lived across the street.

⇥ 16 ⇤

One Last Victory

A crowd of people gathered on a hilltop. Before them stood a long white building, its front lined with a wide porch and many windows. A cold wind swirled around the people, but no one seemed to notice its icy breath. The sun shone, making sparkles on the frost-covered yard.

The crowd climbed the stairs to the porch and then, one by one, they entered the building.

Susan stood in the doorway and greeted them. She recognized every one of the smiling faces. There was Dr. William Ream, a local physician; Charles Cadman, a famous musical composer; and many leaders from the Presbyterian and Quaker Churches. Susan's family was there, as well as her friends and neighbors in Walthill.

Everyone of them had helped – in some way, great and small – to make Susan's dream come true. They helped her raise the money for the building and medical equipment of the new Walthill Hospital.

It was January 8, 1913, the hospital's opening day. Susan had hoped for a reservation hospital ever since her days in medical school. Originally planners considered limiting the hospital to Indians but so many people – from as far away as Pennsylvania – had donated money and time to its construction that it was open to all races.

Susan guided everyone on a tour of the new building. They walked through the two, 12-bed wards; the maternity ward; the five private wards; the operating room and the kitchen. All around the two-story hospital were tall windows that let in sunlight

The Dr. Susan LaFlesche Picotte Memorial Hospital in Walthill, Nebraska. The building was placed on the National Register of Historic Places in 1989.

and fresh air – nature's medicine, Susan said. That's why she'd insisted on building a wide, screened-in porch, where patients could spend some of their recovery time.

Susan still made house calls. But now that people could come to the hospital, she could spend more time with her patients rather than travel for long hours from house to house.

For almost two years Susan continued working as a doctor and counselor – some said she was the unofficial chief of her people, just as her father had been. She was a doctor to her people but she had become much more. She translated legal documents and settled disputes and oversaw financial matters. She was a preacher and teacher. She wrote articles about farming, community health and Omaha traditions. She took food to the needy and cooked meals for the infirm. She healed the sick and comforted the dying. She tended to physical and spiritual needs – the two were as intertwined as the threads in an Omaha blanket, Susan believed. Still there was much more to do. She once told a friend, "The Omahas depend on me so, and I just have to take care of myself till this fight is over."

But in 1915 Susan's heath failed. The pain in her ears and head was diagnosed as "decay of the bone." In the early part of the year she had two operations, but they were unsuccessful. Susan died on September 18.

Thousands of people mourned. Telegrams of grief poured into Walthill. Newspaper articles in Nebraska and other parts of the country expressed sorrow and praised her great work. The *New York Sun* said, "Her word was higher law in the tribe than that of the Indian Agent."

The Omaha Indians lost one of their best friends. It was estimated that in the tribe of more than 2,000 people, Dr. Sue had treated every member, saving the lives of hundreds of both Indians and white people.

Susan's funeral was simple. Friends and family gathered in her living room around the casket. Three clergymen conducted the service. An elderly Indian gave the final prayer. He spoke in Omaha, the ancient language of her people. Susan would have liked that.

J.L. Wilkerson, a native of Kentucky, now lives in Kansas City, Missouri. A former teacher, Wilkerson has worked as a writer and editor for 25 years. She is an award-winning writer whose essays and articles have appeared in professional journals and popular magazines in the United States and Great Britian. She is the author of several regional history books. Wilkerson has also written children's books, including other biographies for Acorn Books' The Great Heartlanders Series.

ACORN BOOKS
THE GREAT HEARTLANDERS SERIES

You can find this book and other Great Heartlanders books at your local fine bookstores.

For information about school rates for books and educational materials in THE GREAT HEARTLANDERS SERIES contact

Acorn Books
THE GREAT HEARTLANDERS SERIES
7337 Terrace
Kansas City, MO 64114-1256

Other biographies in the series include:
Scribe of the Great Plains: Mari Sandoz
Champion of Arbor Day: J. Sterling Morton
A Doctor to Her People: Dr. Susan LaFlesche Picotte

Additional education materials in THE GREAT HEARTLANDERS SERIES are

- ♦ Activities Books
- ♦ Maps
- ♦ Celebration Kits
- ♦ "Factoid" Bookmarks

To receive a free Great Heartlanders catalog and a complete list of series books and educational materials, write or call Acorn Books.

Toll Free: 1-888-422-0320-READ